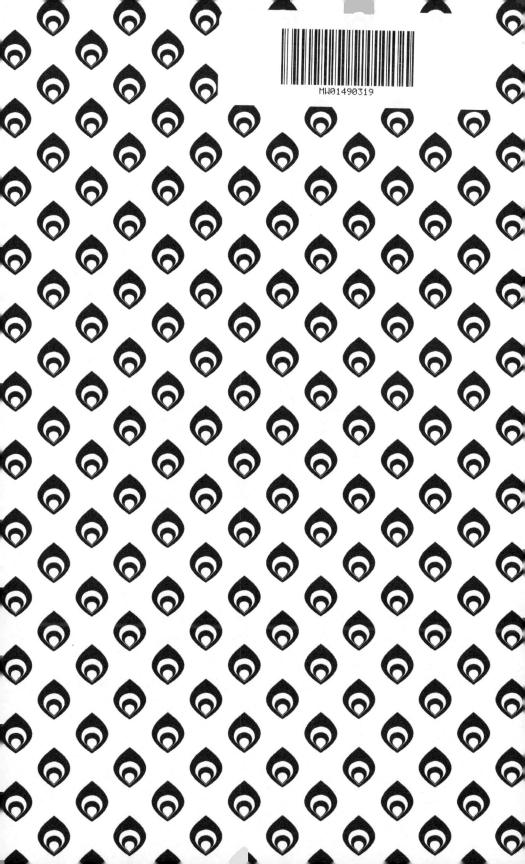

VISIT US ONLINE
CRAZYTIREDBEETCHES.COM

INSTAGRAM
@CRAZYTIREDBEETCHES

Part of the "Cuss Words Make Me Happy™" Series of Journals, Planners and Books by Crazy Tired Beetches™.
Visit Crazy Tired Beetches™ online: www.crazytiredbeetches.com | email us: feedback@crazytiredbeetches.com

FUCK THIS SHIT SHOW: A GRATITUDE JOURNAL FOR TIRED-ASS HUMANS

FIRST EDITION

ISBN: 978-1798869062

CRAZY TIRED BEETCHES PUBLISHING CO LLC
304 South Jones Blvd, #212
Las Vegas, NV 89107

www.crazytiredbeetches.com
feedback@crazytiredbeetches.com

THIS
GRATITUDE JOURNAL
BELONGS TO

ANDREA Jean Czapiewski

🖕 🖕 🖕 🖕 🖕 🖕 🖕 🖕 🖕 🖕

NOW – FUCK OFF...

DATE: 1/5/2020

ASSHOLES ARE EVERYWHERE

HOW DID THEY FUCK WITH YOU TODAY?

No stimulus check deposit!

IT WASN'T ALL BAD BECAUSE...

I read some of my Book and enjoyed Tropical Smoothie w/ Liliana!

HOW I REDEEMED THE DAY

Yoga and a nap!

MY MOOD TODAY

Undo the anger,
release it from
your inner being,
Invite the positivity
in and embrace
it wholly

BEING
PISSED OFF
GETS OLD.
I'M AT A
WHOLE NEW
LEVEL
OF FUCK IT!

Random Moment
I WANT TO KEEP

Helping the neighbor by taking cranberry
juice to her daughter. My friend Tiffany

ASSHOLE OF THE DAY

my horse. She was a complete spass today while giving her hay and well She was not being a good listener.

ONE THING I AM PROUD OF DOING TODAY

I opened up completely in counseling about what I went out of my marriage

SOMETHING THAT REALLY PISSED ME OFF TODAY

My husband said "I don't care, I can't do it" when I told him I had a parent meeting for dance when our neighbor was coming over.

MY MOOD TODAY

GOTTA HAVE GOALS
ARE YOU PROGRESSING?

Yoga Everyday!

Day 27 of plank challenge And 8th straight day of yoga- fit & slim body II.

RANDOM THOUGHTS AND FUCKERY

Schedule Bradys 13 year old pictures,

Get a promotion

Never have to log into instant messaging again.

This is my fucking jam

Schitt's creek hilarity. Love the storyline, and Dan Levy is a soul I could spend hours talking to ... I think, lol!

Football Wild Card Saturday is coming...

DATE: _____

Day of the Week

S M T W TH F S

WHAT KIND OF SHIT
WAS THIS?

I AM PROUD I DIDN'T DO THIS TODAY	I FEEL GRATEFUL FOR THIS TODAY

MY MOOD TODAY

TODAY'S SHIT LIST
PEOPLE, PLACES OR THINGS

DOODLE SOME SHIT HERE

I've got this...
SO FUCK OFF

DATE: _____

I'VE GOT AN ATTITUDE
OF GRATITUDE

I ROCKED THIS TODAY	MAYBE THIS WASN'T MY FINEST MOMENT...

MY MOOD TODAY

TODAY'S SHIT LIST
PEOPLE, PLACES OR THINGS

WHAT'S ON MY MIND

- ☐ HAPPINESS
- ☐ TO BE LEFT THE FUCK ALONE
- ☐ A BIG ASS CUP OF COFFEE
- ☐ REVENGE
- ☐ GRATITUDE
- ☐ NOTHING
- ☐ OTHER:

Now Let That Shit Go...
FUCKING RANT ABOUT IT

DATE: _____

Day of the Week

S M T W TH F S

ASSHOLES ARE EVERYWHERE

HOW DID THEY FUCK WITH YOU TODAY?

IT WASN'T ALL BAD BECAUSE...

HOW I REDEEMED THE DAY

MY MOOD TODAY

TODAY'S LIFE LESSON

I HOPE ONE
DAY YOU CHOKE
ON THE SHIT
YOU TALK.

Random Moment
OF TRUE HAPPINESS

DATE: _____

Day of the Week

S M T W TH F S

WHAT KIND OF SHIT
WAS THIS?

I AM PROUD I DIDN'T DO THIS TODAY

I FEEL GRATEFUL FOR THIS TODAY

MY MOOD TODAY

TODAY'S SHIT LIST

PEOPLE, PLACES OR THINGS

DOODLE SOME SHIT HERE

I've got this...
SO FUCK OFF

DATE: _____

I'VE GOT AN ATTITUDE
OF GRATITUDE

I ROCKED THIS
TODAY

MAYBE THIS WASN'T MY
FINEST MOMENT...

MY MOOD TODAY

TODAY'S SHIT LIST
PEOPLE, PLACES OR THINGS

WHAT'S ON MY MIND

- ☐ HAPPINESS
- ☐ TO BE LEFT THE FUCK ALONE
- ☐ A BIG ASS CUP OF COFFEE
- ☐ REVENGE
- ☐ GRATITUDE
- ☐ NOTHING
- ☐ OTHER:

Now Let That Shit Go...
FUCKING RANT ABOUT IT

DATE: _____

S M T W TH F S

Day of the Week

ASSHOLES ARE EVERYWHERE

HOW DID THEY FUCK WITH YOU TODAY?

IT WASN'T ALL BAD BECAUSE...

HOW I REDEEMED THE DAY

MY MOOD TODAY

REVENGE IS
NOT IN MY
PLANS.
YOU'LL FUCK
YOURSELF
ON YOUR
OWN.

Random Moment

I TOLD SOMEONE TO GO FUCK THEMSELF

DATE: _____

Day of the Week

S M T W TH F S

ASS HOLE OF THE DAY

ONE THING I AM PROUD OF DOING TODAY

SOMETHING THAT REALLY PISSED ME OFF TODAY

MY MOOD TODAY

GOTTA HAVE GOALS
ARE YOU PROGRESSING?

RANDOM THOUGHTS AND FUCKERY

I just bought this
AND FUCKING LOVE IT

DATE: _____

WHAT KIND OF SHIT
WAS THIS?

I AM PROUD I DIDN'T DO THIS TODAY

I FEEL GRATEFUL FOR THIS TODAY

MY MOOD TODAY

TODAY'S SHIT LIST
PEOPLE, PLACES OR THINGS

DOODLE SOME SHIT HERE

I've got this...
SO FUCK OFF

DATE: _____

Day of the Week

S M T W TH F S

I'VE GOT AN ATTITUDE
OF GRATITUDE

I ROCKED THIS TODAY	MAYBE THIS WASN'T MY FINEST MOMENT...

MY MOOD TODAY

TODAY'S SHIT LIST
PEOPLE, PLACES OR THINGS

WHAT'S ON MY MIND

- ☐ HAPPINESS
- ☐ TO BE LEFT THE FUCK ALONE
- ☐ A BIG ASS CUP OF COFFEE
- ☐ REVENGE
- ☐ GRATITUDE
- ☐ NOTHING
- ☐ OTHER:

Now Let That Shit Go...
FUCKING RANT ABOUT IT

DATE: _____

Day of the Week

S M T W TH F S

ASSHOLES ARE EVERYWHERE

HOW DID THEY FUCK WITH YOU TODAY?

IT WASN'T ALL BAD BECAUSE...

HOW I REDEEMED THE DAY

MY MOOD TODAY

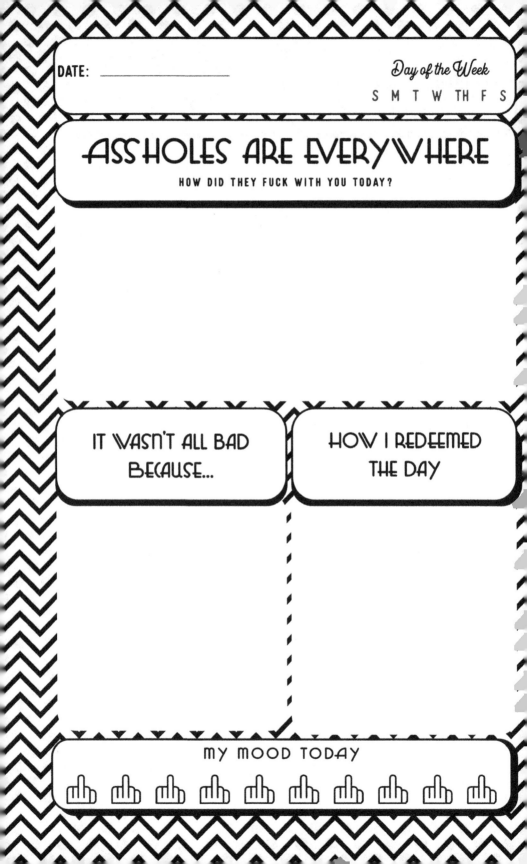

TODAY'S LIFE LESSON

THE KEY TO
HAPPINESS:
STAY AWAY
FROM
ASSHOLES

Random Moment
I FUCKED WITH SOMEONE

DATE: _____

ASSHOLE OF THE DAY

ONE THING I AM PROUD OF DOING TODAY

SOMETHING THAT REALLY PISSED ME OFF TODAY

MY MOOD TODAY

GOTTA HAVE GOALS
ARE YOU PROGRESSING?

RANDOM THOUGHTS AND FUCKERY

Bucket List

DATE: _____

WHAT KIND OF SHIT
WAS THIS?

I AM PROUD I DIDN'T DO THIS TODAY	I FEEL GRATEFUL FOR THIS TODAY

MY MOOD TODAY

TODAY'S SHIT LIST

PEOPLE, PLACES OR THINGS

DOODLE SOME SHIT HERE

I've got this...
SO FUCK OFF

DATE: _____

I'VE GOT AN ATTITUDE
OF GRATITUDE

I ROCKED THIS TODAY	MAYBE THIS WASN'T MY FINEST MOMENT...

MY MOOD TODAY

TODAY'S SHIT LIST
PEOPLE, PLACES OR THINGS

WHAT'S ON MY MIND

- ☐ HAPPINESS
- ☐ TO BE LEFT THE FUCK ALONE
- ☐ A BIG ASS CUP OF COFFEE
- ☐ REVENGE
- ☐ GRATITUDE
- ☐ NOTHING
- ☐ OTHER:

Now Let That Shit Go...
FUCKING RANT ABOUT IT

DATE: _____

Day of the Week

S M T W TH F S

ASSHOLES ARE EVERYWHERE

HOW DID THEY FUCK WITH YOU TODAY?

IT WASN'T ALL BAD BECAUSE...

HOW I REDEEMED THE DAY

MY MOOD TODAY

FEED YOUR
OWN EGO.
I'M BUSY.

Random Moment
I WASN'T A SELFISH PRICK

DATE: _____

Day of the Week

S M T W TH F S

ASSHOLE OF THE DAY

ONE THING I AM PROUD OF DOING TODAY

SOMETHING THAT REALLY PISSED ME OFF TODAY

MY MOOD TODAY

GOTTA HAVE GOALS
ARE YOU PROGRESSING?

RANDOM THOUGHTS AND FUCKERY

Clear your mind clutter

DATE: _____

Day of the Week

S M T W TH F S

WHAT KIND OF SHIT
WAS THIS?

I AM PROUD I DIDN'T DO THIS TODAY	I FEEL GRATEFUL FOR THIS TODAY

MY MOOD TODAY

TODAY'S SHIT LIST
PEOPLE, PLACES OR THINGS

DOODLE SOME SHIT HERE

I've got this...
SO FUCK OFF

DATE: _____

I'VE GOT AN ATTITUDE
OF GRATITUDE

I ROCKED THIS TODAY	MAYBE THIS WASN'T MY FINEST MOMENT...

MY MOOD TODAY

TODAY'S SHIT LIST
PEOPLE, PLACES OR THINGS

WHAT'S ON MY MIND

- ☐ HAPPINESS
- ☐ TO BE LEFT THE FUCK ALONE
- ☐ A BIG ASS CUP OF COFFEE
- ☐ REVENGE
- ☐ GRATITUDE
- ☐ NOTHING
- ☐ OTHER:

Now Let That Shit Go...
FUCKING RANT ABOUT IT

DATE: _____

Day of the Week

S M T W TH F S

ASSHOLES ARE EVERYWHERE

HOW DID THEY FUCK WITH YOU TODAY?

IT WASN'T ALL BAD BECAUSE...

HOW I REDEEMED THE DAY

MY MOOD TODAY

TODAY'S LIFE LESSON

I WOULD
SLAP YOU,
BUT
SHIT
SPLATTERS

Random Moment
TO REMEMBER

DATE: _____

Day of the Week

S M T W TH F S

ASSHOLE OF THE DAY

ONE THING I AM PROUD OF DOING TODAY

SOMETHING THAT REALLY PISSED ME OFF TODAY

MY MOOD TODAY

GOTTA HAVE GOALS
ARE YOU PROGRESSING?

RANDOM THOUGHTS AND FUCKERY

Unrealistic Expectation

DATE: _____

WHAT KIND OF SHIT
WAS THIS?

I AM PROUD I
DIDN'T DO THIS TODAY

I FEEL GRATEFUL
FOR THIS TODAY

MY MOOD TODAY

TODAY'S SHIT LIST
PEOPLE, PLACES OR THINGS

DOODLE SOME SHIT HERE

I've got this...
SO FUCK OFF

DATE: _____

Day of the Week

S M T W TH F S

I'VE GOT AN ATTITUDE
OF GRATITUDE

I ROCKED THIS TODAY

MAYBE THIS WASN'T MY FINEST MOMENT...

MY MOOD TODAY

TODAY'S SHIT LIST
PEOPLE, PLACES OR THINGS

WHAT'S ON MY MIND

- ☐ HAPPINESS
- ☐ TO BE LEFT THE FUCK ALONE
- ☐ A BIG ASS CUP OF COFFEE
- ☐ REVENGE
- ☐ GRATITUDE
- ☐ NOTHING
- ☐ OTHER:

Now Let That Shit Go...
FUCKING RANT ABOUT IT

DATE: _____

ASSHOLES ARE EVERYWHERE

HOW DID THEY FUCK WITH YOU TODAY?

IT WASN'T ALL BAD BECAUSE...

HOW I REDEEMED THE DAY

MY MOOD TODAY

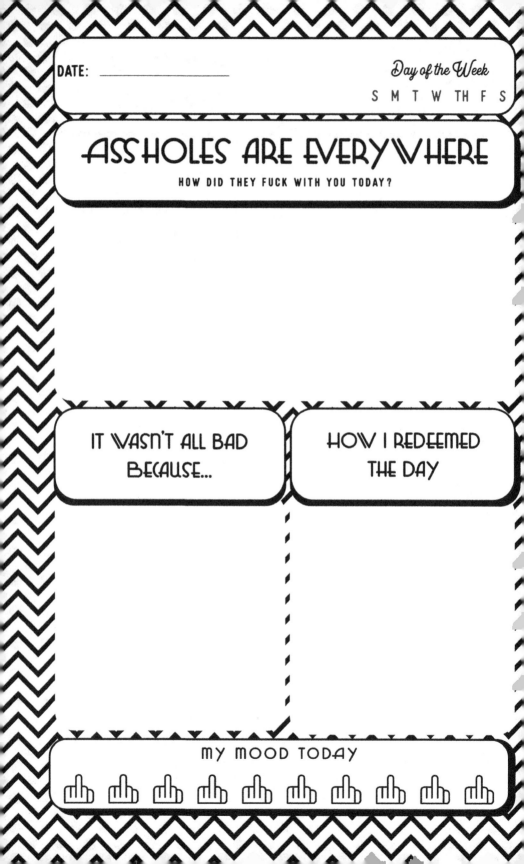

ONLY DEAD FISH
GO WITH THE
FLOW

Random Moment

I GAVE SOMEONE THE FINGER

DATE: _____

ASSHOLE OF THE DAY

ONE THING I AM PROUD OF DOING TODAY

SOMETHING THAT REALLY PISSED ME OFF TODAY

MY MOOD TODAY

GOTTA HAVE GOALS
ARE YOU PROGRESSING?

RANDOM THOUGHTS AND FUCKERY

I'm Ignoring This Goal

DATE: _____

WHAT KIND OF SHIT
WAS THIS?

I AM PROUD I DIDN'T DO THIS TODAY

I FEEL GRATEFUL FOR THIS TODAY

MY MOOD TODAY

TODAY'S SHIT LIST
PEOPLE, PLACES OR THINGS

DOODLE
SOME SHIT HERE

I've got this...
SO FUCK OFF

DATE: _____

Day of the Week

S M T W TH F S

I'VE GOT AN ATTITUDE
OF GRATITUDE

I ROCKED THIS TODAY	MAYBE THIS WASN'T MY FINEST MOMENT...

MY MOOD TODAY

TODAY'S SHIT LIST
PEOPLE, PLACES OR THINGS

WHAT'S ON MY MIND

- ☐ HAPPINESS
- ☐ TO BE LEFT THE FUCK ALONE
- ☐ A BIG ASS CUP OF COFFEE
- ☐ REVENGE
- ☐ GRATITUDE
- ☐ NOTHING
- ☐ OTHER:

Now Let That Shit Go...
FUCKING RANT ABOUT IT

DATE: _____

ASSHOLES ARE EVERYWHERE

HOW DID THEY FUCK WITH YOU TODAY?

IT WASN'T ALL BAD BECAUSE...

HOW I REDEEMED THE DAY

MY MOOD TODAY

TODAY'S LIFE LESSON

I DON'T
TAKE ORDERS.
I BARELY
TAKE
SUGGESTIONS.

Random Moment
I DRANK TOO MUCH

DATE: _____

Day of the Week

S M T W TH F S

ASS HOLE OF THE DAY

ONE THING I AM PROUD OF DOING TODAY

SOMETHING THAT REALLY PISSED ME OFF TODAY

MY MOOD TODAY

GOTTA HAVE GOALS
ARE YOU PROGRESSING?

RANDOM THOUGHTS AND FUCKERY

Bills You Wish
WOULD DISAPPEAR

DATE: _____

Day of the Week

S M T W TH F S

WHAT KIND OF SHIT
WAS THIS?

I AM PROUD I
DIDN'T DO THIS TODAY

I FEEL GRATEFUL
FOR THIS TODAY

MY MOOD TODAY

TODAY'S SHIT LIST
PEOPLE, PLACES OR THINGS

DOODLE SOME SHIT HERE

I've got this...
SO FUCK OFF

DATE: _____

I'VE GOT AN ATTITUDE
OF GRATITUDE

I ROCKED THIS TODAY	MAYBE THIS WASN'T MY FINEST MOMENT...

MY MOOD TODAY

TODAY'S SHIT LIST
PEOPLE, PLACES OR THINGS

WHAT'S ON MY MIND

- ☐ HAPPINESS
- ☐ TO BE LEFT THE FUCK ALONE
- ☐ A BIG ASS CUP OF COFFEE
- ☐ REVENGE
- ☐ GRATITUDE
- ☐ NOTHING
- ☐ OTHER:

Now Let That Shit Go...
FUCKING RANT ABOUT IT

DATE: _____

Day of the Week

S M T W TH F S

ASSHOLES ARE EVERYWHERE

HOW DID THEY FUCK WITH YOU TODAY?

IT WASN'T ALL BAD BECAUSE...

HOW I REDEEMED THE DAY

MY MOOD TODAY

"FUCK THAT SHIT" IS A PERFECTLY ACCEPTABLE SUBSTITUTE FOR THE WORD "NO"

Random Moment

TO NEVER SPEAK OF AGAIN

DATE: _____

Day of the Week

S M T W TH F S

WHAT KIND OF SHIT
WAS THIS?

I AM PROUD I DIDN'T DO THIS TODAY

I FEEL GRATEFUL FOR THIS TODAY

MY MOOD TODAY

TODAY'S SHIT LIST
PEOPLE, PLACES OR THINGS

DOODLE
SOME SHIT HERE

I've got this...
SO FUCK OFF

DATE: _____

Day of the Week

S M T W TH F S

ASSHOLE OF THE DAY

ONE THING I AM PROUD
OF DOING TODAY

SOMETHING THAT REALLY
PISSED ME OFF TODAY

MY MOOD TODAY

GOTTA HAVE GOALS
ARE YOU PROGRESSING?

RANDOM THOUGHTS AND FUCKERY

Why The Fuck...
DID I EAT THAT?

DATE: _____

Day of the Week

S M T W TH F S

ASSHOLES ARE EVERYWHERE

HOW DID THEY FUCK WITH YOU TODAY?

IT WASN'T ALL BAD BECAUSE...

HOW I REDEEMED THE DAY

MY MOOD TODAY

TODAY'S LIFE LESSON

I SHOULD BE
GIVEN A FUCKING
AWARD
FOR KEEPING
MY MOUTH
SHUT
WHEN THERE IS
SO MUCH SHIT
THAT NEEDS
TO BE SAID

Random Moment
I WAS ANYTHING BUT CALM

DATE: _____

Day of the Week

S M T W TH F S

WHAT KIND OF SHIT
WAS THIS?

I AM PROUD I
DIDN'T DO THIS TODAY

I FEEL GRATEFUL
FOR THIS TODAY

MY MOOD TODAY

TODAY'S SHIT LIST
PEOPLE, PLACES OR THINGS

DOODLE SOME SHIT HERE

I've got this...
SO FUCK OFF

DATE: _____

I'VE GOT AN ATTITUDE
OF GRATITUDE

I ROCKED THIS TODAY	MAYBE THIS WASN'T MY FINEST MOMENT...

MY MOOD TODAY

TODAY'S SHIT LIST
PEOPLE, PLACES OR THINGS

WHAT'S ON MY MIND

- ☐ HAPPINESS
- ☐ TO BE LEFT THE FUCK ALONE
- ☐ A BIG ASS CUP OF COFFEE
- ☐ REVENGE
- ☐ GRATITUDE
- ☐ NOTHING
- ☐ OTHER:

Now Let That Shit Go...
FUCKING RANT ABOUT IT

DATE: _____

Day of the Week

S M T W TH F S

ASSHOLES ARE EVERYWHERE

HOW DID THEY FUCK WITH YOU TODAY?

IT WASN'T ALL BAD BECAUSE...

HOW I REDEEMED THE DAY

MY MOOD TODAY

TODAY'S LIFE LESSON

I'M SMILING
BECAUSE I KNOW
KARMA
WILL
BITCH-SLAP
YOU
EVENTUALLY

Random Moment

I MADE UP

DATE: _____

Day of the Week
S M T W TH F S

ASS HOLE OF THE DAY

ONE THING I AM PROUD OF DOING TODAY

SOMETHING THAT REALLY PISSED ME OFF TODAY

MY MOOD TODAY

GOTTA HAVE GOALS
ARE YOU PROGRESSING?

RANDOM THOUGHTS AND FUCKERY

Bitch, please...

DATE: _____

Day of the Week

S M T W TH F S

I'VE GOT AN ATTITUDE
OF GRATITUDE

I ROCKED THIS TODAY

MAYBE THIS WASN'T MY FINEST MOMENT...

MY MOOD TODAY

TODAY'S SHIT LIST
PEOPLE, PLACES OR THINGS

WHAT'S ON MY MIND

- ☐ HAPPINESS
- ☐ TO BE LEFT THE FUCK ALONE
- ☐ A BIG ASS CUP OF COFFEE
- ☐ REVENGE
- ☐ GRATITUDE
- ☐ NOTHING
- ☐ OTHER:

Now Let That Shit Go...
FUCKING RANT ABOUT IT

DATE: _____

Day of the Week

S M T W TH F S

ASSHOLES ARE EVERYWHERE

HOW DID THEY FUCK WITH YOU TODAY?

IT WASN'T ALL BAD BECAUSE...

HOW I REDEEMED THE DAY

MY MOOD TODAY

I'M NOT
ARGUING.
I'M EXPLAINING
WHY I'M
FUCKING
RIGHT

Random Moment
THAT MADE ME SAD

DATE: _____

WHAT KIND OF SHIT
WAS THIS?

I AM PROUD I
DIDN'T DO THIS TODAY

I FEEL GRATEFUL
FOR THIS TODAY

MY MOOD TODAY

TODAY'S SHIT LIST

PEOPLE, PLACES OR THINGS

DOODLE SOME SHIT HERE

I've got this...
SO FUCK OFF

DATE: _____

Day of the Week

S   M   T   W   TH   F   S

ASSHOLE OF THE DAY

ONE THING I AM PROUD
OF DOING TODAY

SOMETHING THAT REALLY
PISSED ME OFF TODAY

MY MOOD TODAY

GOTTA HAVE GOALS
ARE YOU PROGRESSING?

RANDOM THOUGHTS AND FUCKERY

Plant a Garden
WHAT FUCKING GROWS?

DATE: _____

ASSHOLES ARE EVERYWHERE

HOW DID THEY FUCK WITH YOU TODAY?

IT WASN'T ALL BAD BECAUSE...

HOW I REDEEMED THE DAY

MY MOOD TODAY

TODAY'S LIFE LESSON

SARCASM:
THE ABILITY
TO INSULT
IDIOTS
WITHOUT THEM
REALIZING IT

Random Moment
I SPENT TOO MUCH MONEY

DATE: _____

Day of the Week

S M T W TH F S

ASSHOLE OF THE DAY

ONE THING I AM PROUD OF DOING TODAY

SOMETHING THAT REALLY PISSED ME OFF TODAY

MY MOOD TODAY

GOTTA HAVE GOALS
ARE YOU PROGRESSING?

RANDOM THOUGHTS AND FUCKERY

This is one person
I TRULY FUCKING LOVE

DATE: _____

Day of the Week

S M T W TH F S

WHAT KIND OF SHIT
WAS THIS?

I AM PROUD I
DIDN'T DO THIS TODAY

I FEEL GRATEFUL
FOR THIS TODAY

MY MOOD TODAY

TODAY'S SHIT LIST
PEOPLE, PLACES OR THINGS

DOODLE
SOME SHIT HERE

I've got this...
SO FUCK OFF

DATE: _____

Day\ of\ the\ Week

S M T W TH F S

I'VE GOT AN ATTITUDE
OF GRATITUDE

I ROCKED THIS TODAY	MAYBE THIS WASN'T MY FINEST MOMENT...

MY MOOD TODAY

TODAY'S SHIT LIST
PEOPLE, PLACES OR THINGS

WHAT'S ON MY MIND

- ☐ HAPPINESS
- ☐ TO BE LEFT THE FUCK ALONE
- ☐ A BIG ASS CUP OF COFFEE
- ☐ REVENGE
- ☐ GRATITUDE
- ☐ NOTHING
- ☐ OTHER:

Now Let That Shit Go...
FUCKING RANT ABOUT IT

DATE: _____

Day of the Week

S M T W TH F S

ASSHOLES ARE EVERYWHERE

HOW DID THEY FUCK WITH YOU TODAY?

IT WASN'T ALL BAD BECAUSE...

HOW I REDEEMED THE DAY

MY MOOD TODAY

DAMMIT I'M MAD
IS
DAMMIT I'M MAD
SPELLED
BACKWARDS
GO AHEAD AND CHECK, ASSHOLE.

Random Moment
I WAS SO FUCKING PROUD

DATE: _____

Day of the Week

S   M   T   W   TH   F   S

ASSHOLE OF THE DAY

ONE THING I AM PROUD OF DOING TODAY

SOMETHING THAT REALLY PISSED ME OFF TODAY

MY MOOD TODAY

GOTTA HAVE GOALS
ARE YOU PROGRESSING?

RANDOM THOUGHTS AND FUCKERY

I did this nice thing today...
BECAUSE I'M FUCKING AMAZING

DATE: _____

Day of the Week

S M T W TH F S

ASSHOLES ARE EVERYWHERE

HOW DID THEY FUCK WITH YOU TODAY?

IT WASN'T ALL BAD BECAUSE...

HOW I REDEEMED THE DAY

MY MOOD TODAY

TODAY'S LIFE LESSON

THERAPY HELPS.
BUT SCREAMING
PROFANITY
IS FASTER
AND
CHEAPER

Random Moment

I WAS GREEDY AS FUCK

DATE: _____

WHAT KIND OF SHIT
WAS THIS?

I AM PROUD I DIDN'T DO THIS TODAY

I FEEL GRATEFUL FOR THIS TODAY

MY MOOD TODAY

TODAY'S SHIT LIST
PEOPLE, PLACES OR THINGS

DOODLE SOME SHIT HERE

I've got this...
SO FUCK OFF

DATE: _____

Day of the Week
S M T W TH F S

ASSHOLES ARE EVERYWHERE
HOW DID THEY FUCK WITH YOU TODAY?

IT WASN'T ALL BAD BECAUSE...

HOW I REDEEMED THE DAY

MY MOOD TODAY

TODAY'S LIFE LESSON

THE OLDER
I GET,
THE MORE
EVERYONE CAN
KISS MY
ASS

Random Moment
TO SHOW I'M A BADASS

DATE: _____

I'VE GOT AN ATTITUDE
OF GRATITUDE

I ROCKED THIS TODAY

MAYBE THIS WASN'T MY FINEST MOMENT...

MY MOOD TODAY

TODAY'S SHIT LIST
PEOPLE, PLACES OR THINGS

WHAT'S ON MY MIND

- ☐ HAPPINESS
- ☐ TO BE LEFT THE FUCK ALONE
- ☐ A BIG ASS CUP OF COFFEE
- ☐ REVENGE
- ☐ GRATITUDE
- ☐ NOTHING
- ☐ OTHER:

Now Let That Shit Go...
FUCKING RANT ABOUT IT

DATE: _____

Day of the Week

S M T W TH F S

ASSHOLES ARE EVERYWHERE

HOW DID THEY FUCK WITH YOU TODAY?

IT WASN'T ALL BAD BECAUSE...

HOW I REDEEMED THE DAY

MY MOOD TODAY

TODAY'S LIFE LESSON

I'LL GET
OVER IT.
I JUST NEED
TO BE
DRAMATIC
FIRST

Random Moment

I ACTED LIKE A DICK

DATE: _____

Day of the Week

S M T W TH F S

ASSHOLE OF THE DAY

ONE THING I AM PROUD
OF DOING TODAY

SOMETHING THAT REALLY
PISSED ME OFF TODAY

MY MOOD TODAY

GOTTA HAVE GOALS
ARE YOU PROGRESSING?

RANDOM THOUGHTS AND FUCKERY

I'm so fucking exhausted
BECAUSE OF THIS

DATE: _____

Day of the Week

S M T W TH F S

ASS HOLE OF THE DAY

ONE THING I AM PROUD OF DOING TODAY	SOMETHING THAT REALLY PISSED ME OFF TODAY

MY MOOD TODAY

GOTTA HAVE GOALS
ARE YOU PROGRESSING?

RANDOM THOUGHTS AND FUCKERY

My mode of transportation
I'D FLY IF I HAD WINGS

DATE: _____

I'VE GOT AN ATTITUDE
OF GRATITUDE

I ROCKED THIS TODAY	MAYBE THIS WASN'T MY FINEST MOMENT...

MY MOOD TODAY

TODAY'S SHIT LIST
PEOPLE, PLACES OR THINGS

WHAT'S ON MY MIND

- ☐ HAPPINESS
- ☐ TO BE LEFT THE FUCK ALONE
- ☐ A BIG ASS CUP OF COFFEE
- ☐ REVENGE
- ☐ GRATITUDE
- ☐ NOTHING
- ☐ OTHER:

Now Let That Shit Go...
FUCKING RANT ABOUT IT

DATE: _____

Day of the Week

S M T W TH F S

ASSHOLES ARE EVERYWHERE

HOW DID THEY FUCK WITH YOU TODAY?

IT WASN'T ALL BAD BECAUSE...

HOW I REDEEMED THE DAY

MY MOOD TODAY

WRITE YOUR OWN
FUCKING QUOTE

Random Moment

OF SUNSHINE AND RAINBOWS

DATE: _____

WHAT KIND OF SHIT
WAS THIS?

I AM PROUD I DIDN'T DO THIS TODAY

I FEEL GRATEFUL FOR THIS TODAY

MY MOOD TODAY

TODAY'S SHIT LIST
PEOPLE, PLACES OR THINGS

DOODLE SOME SHIT HERE

I've got this...
SO FUCK OFF

DATE: _____

Day of the Week

S M T W TH F S

ASSHOLES ARE EVERYWHERE

HOW DID THEY FUCK WITH YOU TODAY?

IT WASN'T ALL BAD BECAUSE...

HOW I REDEEMED THE DAY

MY MOOD TODAY

I CAN FUCKING
EXPLAIN IT TO YOU.
I CAN'T FUCKING
UNDERSTAND IT
FOR YOU.

Random Moment

WRITTEN IN PIG LATIN

DATE: _____

Day of the Week
S M T W TH F S

ASSHOLES ARE EVERYWHERE

HOW DID THEY FUCK WITH YOU TODAY?

IT WASN'T ALL BAD BECAUSE...

HOW I REDEEMED THE DAY

MY MOOD TODAY

NO ONE LOOKS
BACK ON
THEIR LIFE
AND REMEMBERS
THE NIGHTS THEY
GOT PLENTY
OF SLEEP

Random Moment

WHEN I NEARLY SMACKED THE DUDE

DATE: _____

WHAT KIND OF SHIT
WAS THIS?

I AM PROUD I DIDN'T DO THIS TODAY

I FEEL GRATEFUL FOR THIS TODAY

MY MOOD TODAY

TODAY'S SHIT LIST
PEOPLE, PLACES OR THINGS

DOODLE SOME SHIT HERE

I've got this...
SO FUCK OFF

DATE: _____

Day of the Week

S M T W TH F S

ASSHOLES ARE EVERYWHERE

HOW DID THEY FUCK WITH YOU TODAY?

IT WASN'T ALL BAD BECAUSE...

HOW I REDEEMED THE DAY

MY MOOD TODAY

NOT
GIVING A
FUCK
IS BETTER
THAN
REVENGE

Random Moment
OF NOT GIVING A FUCK

DATE: _____

ASS HOLE OF THE DAY

ONE THING I AM PROUD OF DOING TODAY

SOMETHING THAT REALLY PISSED ME OFF TODAY

MY MOOD TODAY

GOTTA HAVE GOALS
ARE YOU PROGRESSING?

RANDOM THOUGHTS AND FUCKERY

Write about
ANYTHING YOU FUCKING WANT

DATE: _____

Day of the Week

S M T W TH F S

I'VE GOT AN ATTITUDE
OF GRATITUDE

I ROCKED THIS TODAY

MAYBE THIS WASN'T MY FINEST MOMENT...

MY MOOD TODAY

TODAY'S SHIT LIST
PEOPLE, PLACES OR THINGS

WHAT'S ON MY MIND

- ☐ HAPPINESS
- ☐ TO BE LEFT THE FUCK ALONE
- ☐ A BIG ASS CUP OF COFFEE
- ☐ REVENGE
- ☐ GRATITUDE
- ☐ NOTHING
- ☐ OTHER:

Now Let That Shit Go...
FUCKING RANT ABOUT IT

DATE: _____

Day of the Week
S M T W TH F S

ASSHOLES ARE EVERYWHERE
HOW DID THEY FUCK WITH YOU TODAY?

IT WASN'T ALL BAD BECAUSE...

HOW I REDEEMED THE DAY

MY MOOD TODAY

I'M TRYING
TO SEE THINGS
FROM YOUR
POINT OF VIEW,
BUT I CAN'T
STICK MY HEAD
THAT FAR
UP MY ASS

Random Moment

I WAS A JERK AS A KID

DATE: _____

ASSHOLES ARE EVERYWHERE

HOW DID THEY FUCK WITH YOU TODAY?

IT WASN'T ALL BAD BECAUSE...

HOW I REDEEMED THE DAY

MY MOOD TODAY

TODAY'S LIFE LESSON

HAVING A
DIRTY MIND
MAKES
ORDINARY
CONVERSATIONS
SO MUCH MORE
INTERESTING

Random Moment

I FELL IN LOVE WITH

THE BEETCHES STORY

Crazy Tired Beetches™ is a small, woman-owned company that publishes unique and fun planners, journals and gifts. We believe that cuss words can make you happy, and we are simply a group of women who enjoy laughing at life.

Our journals, planners and calendars are designed for women to pick up, giggle, and share a laugh with their friends, family and colleagues. We are a little bit snarky, a little bit sassy, and a whole lot of fun!

We may cuss (a TON), but we find sometimes a few strategically placed F-Bombs make the stress and insanity of everyday life laughable, and a heck of a lot more enjoyable!

With that, we hope you find a giggle, belly laugh or just smile at our collection of products. If you do, we would love it if you would leave us a review on Amazon!

If you are unhappy, please reach out to us at feedback@crazytiredbeetches.com. .

We are proudly based in the USA and look forward to continuing taking life not too seriously with you!

Yours in Laughter,
THE CTB CREW

www.crazytiredbeetches.com

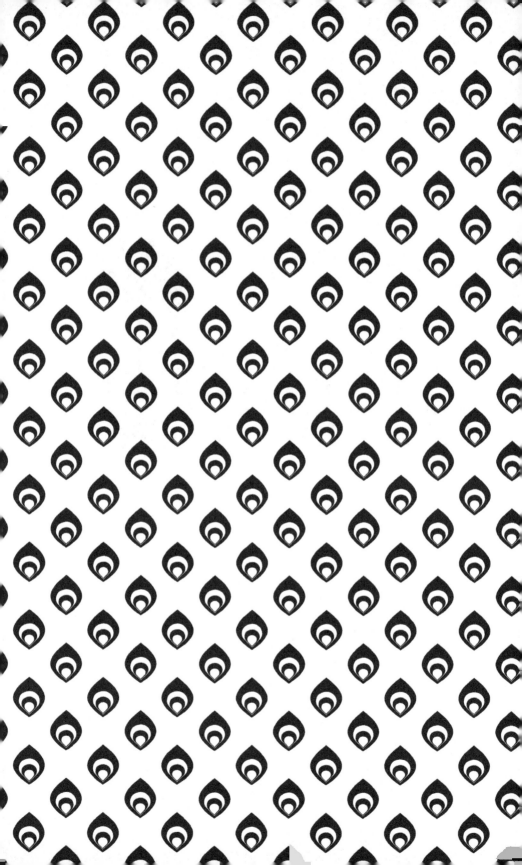

Made in the USA
Monee, IL
19 December 2020